MW00641556

Non-Confrontational
Power Selling

David Jacobson

Non-Confrontational
Power Selling

The Most Effective and Useful Book on Selling Ever Printed

Featuring

The 7 Commandments of Selling

Copyright © 1999 by David Jacobson
All rights reserved. No part of this book may be reproduced or utilized in any form or by any means, including photocopying, recording, or by any information storage or retrieval system, without permission in writing from publisher. Inquires should be addressed to Capital Results, Inc., 414 West Sunrise Hwy., Patchogue, NY 11772. It is the policy of Capital Results, Inc. and its imprints and affiliates in recognizing the importance of preserving what has been written, to print the books we publish on acid free paper, and exert our best efforts to that end.

Library of Congress Catalog Card Number: 98-97015
ISBN: 0-9668974-3-9

Printed In the United States of America

Acknowledgments

I would like to thank and give public praise to the following people:

All of the people that I have come in contact with who, unknowingly through their wisdom and knowledge, have given me opportunities to learn and grow.

Kristine Mason for her loving support in life and with this book. Her drive and determination to achieve personal goals have inspired me greatly.

Ron Stanton, my mentor, for his profound sales ability and teaching which started me in the right direction.

Neil Feldstein, for instilling in me not to accept anything other than my best.

My mother, Anita, for always believing in me and reassuring me that I had the talent to be successful.

My father, Jack, who role modeled that hard work and consistency strengthens the foundation on which you build.

My brother, Howard, for allowing me to tag along with him while growing up. He taught me a great lesson; how teaching and support can help build a strong foundation for your future.

My Daughter Kayla and my son Dylan, through their smiles and laughter I am able to see the lighter side of life.

This book is dedicated to
every salesperson who, in spite of the
odds, through hard work and
determination makes things
happen for themselves.

Contents

Preface

Thank you for purchasing a copy of *Non-Confrontational Power Selling.* Most people who purchase a book of this kind are usually looking become better at what they do for a living, which will result in making more money. The bonus of *Non-Confrontational Power Selling* is that it extends above and beyond this. For instance, **would you like to take the stress out of your job, make more money and have fun doing it? It sounds impossible, doesn't it? In fact, many people would call this Heaven.**

Welcome to the Golden Gates

Many people hear the terms *Non-Confrontational* and *Power Selling* used together and they do not understand how they can coexist. Once you have read this book, you will see exactly how this is possible.

In order for you to reap the full benefits of Non-Confrontational Power Selling, you must make a personal commitment to be open to new ideas and to then implement these ideas. As a result, you will foster the changes necessary to reach the highest levels of personal growth and success.

Over the past twenty years, I have compiled information that is believed by many to be the most effective sales program in the industry today. This valuable compilation is now available to you in an easy to read format; therefore, the rest is up to you. Enjoy your journey of success.

Introduction

Human beings possess many natural instincts. However, as children we don't really understand their true power. The most powerful is our ability to sell. Can you remember as a child convincing your parents to let you sleep over a friend's house? You would let them know your friend's parents would be home and that it was OK. I can recall being about 12 years old and selling my parents on letting me play outside a little longer each night. I would promise my parents that I would do my homework when I came in and that all the other kids were still outside. As children, this happened at least a dozen times a day; selling someone on something. The funny thing is, we were all pretty good at it. Why? It was instinctual. We were very natural and convincing even though we didn't get our way all the time. Eventually our parents caught on.

As we grow older, more often than not, we become manipulators. It is no longer natural to sell someone. This could be because there is more at stake or perhaps because others are more skeptical of us. We all possess the natural ability to be convincing. Unfortunately, it's lost and, therefore, must be relearned. If you can sell with the same passion and emotion you felt as a child and combine it with selling the benefits to your customer today, then you will find the true joy of selling.

When I was thirteen years old, I found some wire on the street, which had been discarded by a telephone repairman. It was the thin wire having about ten different colors. I can remember picking up the wire and taking it home, knowing that I could use it for something.

I played with the wire for a while and then decided to make a colorful ring. I was very excited about my creation and realized I could sell the rings to the kids at school, so I made more. I found some old plastic boxes that a deck of cards might have come in. I displayed the rings in the clear box and brought them to school the next day. I sold my rings for a quarter each and at the end of the day, I made $2.50 and had orders for five more rings. My business flourished throughout the school year.

This experience allowed me to learn early in life that genuine excitement and belief in your product and in yourself are the stepping stones to success.

Over the next ten years, I worked in a retail-clothing store and in the Garment District in New York City.

Since I always had a passion for being on stage, I decided to work with a friend as a mobile disc jockey.

Along my journey of finding myself and my true purpose in life, I met some very sharp people. Some of them had a big impact on the type of salesperson, manager, and trainer I would eventually become.

In 1982, while working as a mobile disc jockey, I decided to change careers. I answered a newspaper ad for auto sales and met the Sales Manager for an interview. He explained to me that very few people make it in the business and most burn out rather quickly. I remember leaving the store with my head spinning. I questioned why anyone would want to work for him (or in the business at all). I forgot the idea immediately.

Two years later, while still working as a mobile disc jockey, I was doing a party for the owner of a dealership on Long Island, New York. It was his 30th birthday. As I was setting up my equipment, we started talking. He asked me if I had ever considered selling cars. I told him of my previous experience at the auto dealership a few years ago. He ultimately persuaded me to meet with his General Manager for an interview a few days later.

The manager was extremely enthusiastic and excited about his job. He painted a completely different picture than the gentleman I had met years before. He explained how the business could be fun and fulfilling. I accepted the job and started a few days later.

My first day happened to fall on President's weekend and the store was packed. All the manager said to me was, "go for it." So I began helping customers and, although the scene was chaotic, I enjoyed it.

I was shocked, as I am now looking back, that they offered no training at all. It was all up to me. I had to take it upon myself to listen and learn. My only teacher was trial and error.

I worked at that particular dealership for three years and during that time I gained priceless experiences that I would take with me into all my future endeavors.

I was now ready to move on and my learning process continued. In 1987, I began my employment at a second dealership. Despite the numerous training courses and seminars I attended, I found true success in confronting the real world challenges of sales that I faced each day. Learning from my mistakes and developing strategies for overcoming obstacles were two of my goals. My intention in writing this book is to share my experiences so that you may reach the goals you have set for yourself.

*"Take things into your own hands
if you want to take advantage
of all the opportunities
that come your way"*

Unfortunately, there is a great lack of training today, both in quality and affordability. Patience is low, demand is high, and support is limited.

If you are going to reach your goals as a salesperson and take advantage of the great opportunities that surround you every day, you need to take things into your own hands. This book will be your resource for doing so.

This book will provide you with solutions to the most difficult situations and circumstances. Based on the real world challenges that sales people face every day, these strategic solutions are proven to be successful.

Non-Confrontational Power Selling is so effective; it will immediately have an impact on your bottom line. Whether it is used as a tool for a single salesperson or as a training guide for a sales team or organization, you will obtain results from the moment you begin implementing the ideas presented. The key is to practice and make the tool verbiage in this book part of your presentation on a consistent basis.

The Business of Sales

The Business of Sales

The automobile business could be considered a strange industry. For example, a customer usually spends an average of twenty minutes traveling to your store and then spends the next twenty minutes trying to leave. What a crazy concept!

Traditionally, sales people usually spend the first few minutes with a customer trying to qualify them. In most cases, this makes customers feel anxious. This anxiety can be displayed in various ways. For instance, I have seen customers walk away from sales people in the middle of a sentence. I have witnessed fights on the showroom floor between customers and sales people and the verbal abuse I have heard is shocking. Sales people spend hours with a customer and then hear the dreaded words, *"Let us think about it."* I often question why a customer, who is about to embark on one of the most exciting purchases of his or her life, would make it such a horrible experience for themselves.

The big questions to ask are, *who is responsible for how a customer feels, who is responsible for how a customer reacts, and who is responsible for the ultimate actions of the customer?*

If you believe customers are responsible for their own actions, you are mistaken. It is inevitable that you will be the one who sets the pace and the tone of the sale by how well you communicate with the customer. This is why it is imperative to understand the various personalities you will encounter, as well as, how to deal with them.

Managers must not take for granted that sales people know their product and their competitor's product. Without such knowledge, there is no sale. A new salesperson must take the time to learn whatever it is he or she is selling, not just for informational purposes but because confidence comes from knowledge. You must be confident. Knowing what you are talking about will better enable you to keep the customer's attention. I use the word enable because you need more than product knowledge to keep the customers attention, which we will talk about later.

"Confidence comes from Knowledge."

"Confidence is necessary to keep control of the sale."

Who are you, as a salesperson?

One of the most crucial ingredients necessary for growing, as a salesperson, is to know what type you are. This will help you to recognize where the areas of growth opportunities exist. We all have some areas that need improvement.

We are constantly learning as sales people. This is because we deal with such vast varieties of people and situations each day.

If you had the opportunity to review a highlight film of all the different people and situations you had or will encounter in your sales career, you would be amazed how each are different in so many ways.

Have you ever met a salesperson while shopping, for anything, and were amazed that this person chose a sales career? The fact is that there are many sales people who should not be in sales. They chose this career because of the lack of options available to them. Hence, unqualified people choose the sales industry.

The good news is that if you have the basic essentials for a salesperson, success is only a matter of information and implementation.

Do you have the essentials?

The following are key items you must bring to the table, in order to succeed.

- *Perseverance.* The ability to make things happen, in spite of the odds. To keep going when people around you are failing. Having the inner drive to see it through.
- *Flexibility.* Making the necessary adjustments as needed. Willingness to venture outside your

comfort zone. The ability to communicate with the many different personalities of people.

- *The inner smile.* A pleasant beam that others can feel projected through your eyes.

You must believe in yourself and your ability. Read on and remember one thing. You are in control of your destiny. Luck is the result of hard work, commitment and perseverance. Wouldn't it be wonderful to look back and know that you made the difference?

"Luck, a gift you receive as the result of hard work."

Part I

Disengaging the Force Field

Chapter 1

Disengaging the Force Field

Disengaging the Force Field

What do customers expect when they come to your store? Probably exactly what they get. You meet, greet, and qualify them in attempt to find out their needs and wants from the very beginning.

As with most new sales people, this is what I was taught when I first entered the car business. The problem with this approach is that while you are qualifying, the customer's first instinct is to be standoffish. These two elements do not mix. As a matter of fact, they are like the two poles of a magnet. The harder you try to qualify a customer, the harder they resist. This sounds like a fun job, doesn't it?

Imagine, if you will, being able to read the customer's mind. It is impossible to do this of course, but there is one thing you can count on, with certainty. When you first meet a customer, what he says is probably not what he means. If you can decode what the customer is saying and truly understand what he is really feeling, you will be in a much better situation.

"The harder you try
to qualify a customer,
the harder she will resist."

"Do not give the customer
what she expects...
a sales pitch."

Decoding what the customer really means

Let's try to decode the customer's language for a moment. If a customer says,

"I just want your best price,"

What he most likely means is,

"I am afraid of you and your sales tactics. I just want to be treated fairly."

Some sales people will immediately become defensive. Others will immediately use a sales pitch. Neither works effectively.

Let's decode another common phrase.

"I just want to look around for a while."

What he probably means is,

"If you stay with me, you will try to sell me something and bother me the whole time, just like the last guy did."

Let's make one thing clear. A customer is thinking one thing to himself throughout the whole process, "What's in it for me?" If there is nothing in it for him then you lose. If a customer is listening, they are probably only patronizing you. If they are walking with you, it is most likely only physically. Unless they have something to gain, you are wasting their time, as well as your own.

What if you have an idea that can benefit the customer? You must let her know this before you tell her about it; otherwise her force field is engaged. As a result, your goal becomes to disengage this force field.

Example:

A customer comes into your store and explains she wants to buy a car for $3,000 cash. You have nothing to sell her at that price, so you suggest she put down the $3,000 and finance the rest. She refuses by saying, "No, I really want to pay cash, but thanks anyway." You try to justify why she should finance and she puts up her defenses, or force field.

You go to your manager after the customer leaves and say, "Man, what a waste. That was just another person wanting a $3,000 car. She told me she was in a rush, but that she would be back." This is such a common occurrence that a sharp salesperson would make a lucrative living on this scenario alone.

The first thing you need to do is disengage the customer's force field. This will help you find out the reasons for their actions. There are many reasons a customer may not be honest with you until they feel they can trust you. For instance, maybe this particular customer was embarrassed to tell you that another dealership rejected her credit and she was told she would have to pay cash.

Remember, you'll make no progress fighting the force field. You must disengage it. The first step is to answer the customer's question of, *"What's in it for me?"* If the customer believes they have something to gain by listening to your ideas, then they will. If they feel they have something to gain by spending time with you, then they will.

Try this approach the next time someone tosses you a stumbling block.

"Because I am also here as a consultant, I would like to share some ideas that you might find quite interesting. Sometimes they make sense and sometimes they don't."

This opens the line of communication and allows you to sell from the inside of the customer's force field. More than likely, you will encounter less resistance and more willingness from the customer and therefore be able to confidently introduce other options.

I recently went to the bank to rent a safety deposit box. A bank employee asked if I needed help. In the middle of my telling her why I was there, another woman, working with a different customer, interrupted her. The woman helping me then said I needed to wait for her. After making me wait for fifteen minutes, she then escorted me to the safety deposit boxes and asked for my key.

I responded a bit annoyed, *"What key?"*

She questioned with frustration, *"Aren't you here to get into your box?"*

I replied, *"No, I want to open a box."*

She said, *"Oh, you need to speak with the other woman you first met."*

This woman engaged my force field instead of disengaging it. This is, unfortunately, a very common occurrence in business. Not just in sales, but in all businesses.

Think before responding to a question. This will enable you to find out what will satisfy the customer. Thinking before responding is a conscious choice you must make and practice. In doing so, you can evolve into the true professional you hope to become.

There was a blockbuster movie titled *Independence Day.* The basic plot involved the invasion of Earth by hostile aliens. In the movie, it was only after the humans disengaged the mother ship's force field that they could destroy the enemy.

In this case, fiction does depict reality. The more aggressive the humans were, the angrier the aliens became. As a result, they retaliated with great fury.

The mother ship was the decision-maker. The humans needed to find a way inside the huge mother ship in order to disengage the force field. They needed to find an actual alien ship so they would seem like one of them and not be detected as invaders. Once they found an alien ship and were inside, they moved slowly and carefully so they would not give themselves away. Does this sound familiar?

Your customer needs to believe in you and feel like you truly understand them. This does not happen with sales pitches. It happens by answering their question, *"What's in it for me?"* Focusing on this question enables you to set the pace, stay in control, and make the experience enjoyable for both you and the customer.

"What's in it for me?"

"What do I have to gain
by spending time with you?"

"These are the questions you
must answer for the customer first.
Then you have earned
the right to continue."

Don't scare them

Phrases and terms can scare someone just as much as a situation can and need to be avoided throughout the sale. Do you know what they are? I hear them all the time.

Simply changing words can be the difference between making or breaking a sale. The way you phrase something can influence a customer's thoughts, actions, and decisions. People are affected by how you say something. This is part of human nature.

Start to become aware of your surroundings. Pay close attention throughout your day and observe how people communicate and the mistakes that are made. Notice the communication process and the verbal and nonverbal reactions. Notice how people naturally become defensive. Start to use the tool verbiage and you will begin to encourage more positive behaviors.

There are certain words that should never be used in front of a customer. I refer to them as the **forbidden words.** Examples of such words are **sell** and **afford.** Let's put these words into a commonly used phrase.

"If I can get you to a price you can afford, could I sell you this car?"

If you use this phrase or anything similar, you are losing 50% of your customers. Try this instead.

"If I could possibly make the price more comfortable for you, would that help to earn your business?"

This approach takes the edge off the intimidating question you have asked. Put yourself in the customer's shoes. First of all, how do you know what they can afford? Secondly, they don't want to be sold. Help them make their own decision.

Other forbidden words commonly used are **shopping** or **shopped.** For example,

"How long have you been shopping around?"

"Where else have you shopped?"

Try this instead.

"How long have you been considering buying a new car?

"What brought it to a head?" and *"Why now?"*

The answers to these questions will give you the information you need to proceed.

Remember, your goal is to be a consultant and a friend to the buyer. You need to change the way you perceive the customer. They aren't steaks on the barbecue.

Have you ever gone grocery shopping while you were hungry? You probably wanted to buy everything in sight. You need to eat before you shop so you can think clearly.

The same is true in selling. You must be consistent in the way you approach a sale and not view the sale as a means for survival. You must approach the sale satisfied and content in your ability. This comes across in the terms and phrases you use.

I remember being a new salesperson and feeling as if I had lost when a customer didn't buy. Maybe they didn't like me, or maybe I should have acted differently. This was partially true. But you cannot sell everyone. When you say and do things that you know will hurt your chances, or when you should have gone in one direction and did not, then you should question yourself. If you have done all you can and you have truly learned Non-Confrontational Power Selling, then you say, "Next" and move on.

But, when a mistake is made, learn from it. Don't make the same mistake twice. If you are using words that will scare customers, change them immediately. Successful sales people do make mistakes. The difference is, they learn from them and make the necessary changes.

"It doesn't matter what you say or
how you say it…

how it is interpreted is what counts."

"A person who learns from his or her mistakes is more valuable than someone who has never tried."

Chapter 2

Stop Selling

Stop Selling

I am going to share with you the biggest tool in selling. It is rarely used, yet it is the most effective technique. Since the first two minutes with a customer are so crucial, it is necessary to use the technique with consistency.

The technique is to ***Stop Selling! Stop Pitching!***

Imagine the pressure you would take off yourself if you stopped selling. No pitches, no cliches. Your ultimate goal is to sell your product. However, your immediate goal is to disengage the customer's force field. How do we disengage the force field? Remember, you and the customer have different instincts. You sell and they engage. Until you get inside the mother ship, you must work on disengagement.

If selling is what they expect from you and all it does is engage their force field, **why sell?**

"Two minute warning...

never sell during the first two minutes with a customer."

Let's review some examples

A customer is approaching the showroom. OK, here he comes.

Who's up?

"I am," you say with little enthusiasm, as you approach the customer.

"Hi Folks, I'm Adam and you are?"

"Charlie and Mary," they respond apprehensively.

"How can I help you today?"

"Well, we are just looking."

You have just created an uphill battle and made a usually detrimental error.

What can you say when a customer tells you they are just looking? Anything you say at this point means you either did not understand them or you are being pushy. Most sales people's instinct at this point is to start selling with comments such as the following:

"Well OK, but we have a big sale going on."

The force field is engaged and a typical customer response is,

"Let us look for a while and we'll get you if we need assistance."

I was recently on the Internet surfing through some web sites on sales training. I came across a very clever web site. A company had an online test consisting of fifteen questions, which was then graded upon completion. If you failed the test, they recommended training in a specialized area with their company.

There was one question in particular that asked what you should do after introducing yourself to a customer? They offered four choices; I did not agree with any of them. To find out their correct answer I chose one at random. *"How can I help you today?"*

Most trainers teach sales people not to ask customers questions that can be answered with a yes or no. This is a very good point, however it's not enough. If you ask a customer, *"How can I help you today?"* They will most likely say they are *"Just looking for now, but thanks anyway."*

Such tactics are all too common in sales today. You must break through the nonsense of sales by building a relationship based on **trust** and **emotion.**

While writing this book, I took a break and went into the showroom. I happened to overhear a salesman **stalking** a customer, I mean talking to a customer. He said,

"Well, you need to give me some time so I can get you some prices."

The customer said,

"That's all right, I don't have much time. I'll come back."

The salesman then said,

"Well, we have some good deals. If you have a couple of minutes I'll get you some prices."

The customer was standing at the salesman's desk during this conversation and then abruptly decided to leave.

I have hundreds of these stories. Each time the same mistake is made. The salesperson's instinct is to sell and the customer's instinct is to engage their Force Field.

A salesperson meeting a customer outside on the lot is another example. The first thing a customer is going to ask is for prices. Do you give the prices on the lot or do you avoid answering the questions? Truthfully, you can't do either. You must stay in control and still make them happy, but how? Please read on.

I keep reading and hearing about the nationa
ing ratio. I believe, from experience, that if a salesperson can master this Non-Confrontational Power Selling technique, he or she will close 60-70% of all customers with less stress and more fun. You aren't convinced? The answer is, you won't know until you try.

On the other side, there are great success stories. For example, I recently had the pleasure of helping a customer who, when I introduced myself, responded by saying, *"Hi, I'm not buying a car today."* I then said hello to her husband by saying, *"This must be Mr. I am not buying a car today."* We all laughed and the tension was eased a bit. The customer thought she meant what she said and I accepted her answer and continued getting to know them by using the methods in this book. It turns out her father had recently died and the money he had left her would not be available for about five months. We briefly talked about how she felt about the loss of her father. This helped to bring the customer and me closer. Through building a relationship on strength, trust and control, I leased them a new Buick Century with no money down and I made a customer for life. No sales pitch needed. I gained the respect and trust by overcoming their concerns and nervousness about the process of buying a new car. It was truly a fun experience for both them and me. It is so unfortunate, however that most sales people would have gone a different route. It is so easy to turn this into a typical wasted up, but by using the Non-Confrontational Power Selling techniques it was an all-around success.

Stop selling, find the fork in the road to the sale and help the customer make a wise choice.

Chapter 3

W.I.T.H

W.I.T.H

Welcome... **I**ntroduce... **T**hank... **H**ow did you hear about (our organization)?

Welcome to (our organization). *My name is David and yours? Thank you for coming in today. How did you hear about* (our organization)*?*

Most good sales people will welcome, introduce, and thank. The question *"How did you hear about us?"* Is what is usually missing and this question sets the stage for small talk rather than selling. Find out about the customer. People love to talk about themselves. When you ask how they heard about the organization, they will respond with many answers, such as: they live locally, they were recommended, they are a previous customer, they were driving through town, they saw a newspaper ad, etc. These are great conversation starters. Furthermore, they give you important information you will need during the sale.

At first it feels strange not to sell. But this small talk will help you relate and find a common ground. It will also help you expand your comfort zone.

Most sales people have difficulty selling to people they cannot relate to. Small talk will help you and the customer feel comfortable with one another. However, this shouldn't last for more than one to three minutes.

"How much time did you plan on spending with us today?"

During the 'small talk' you should know the appropriate time to ask this question. But what if the timing never feels right? Sometimes you may find yourself in an awkward situation. The customer may be very shy or have had a bad experience with another salesperson.

Try this the next time you run out of small talk and you haven't found the right opportunity to ask, *"How much time did you plan on spending with us today?"*

"What are you driving now?"

Get them to talk about their car. Follow up with:

"How do you like it?"

"Is this the car you are looking to replace?"

Usually the answers to these questions will open the door for good conversation and provide you with the opportunity to ask...

"How much time did you plan on spending with us today."

The answer will tell you how much time you have left to disengage the force field, if you haven't already done so. It will also bring up legitimate time restraints. No matter what the answer is, it works. If the customer's response is,

"I only have five minutes" or *"I only have one minute"* or *"20 minutes,"*

Your response should be,

"To make the best use of your (customer's response), *let me ask you a few quick questions so I can point **us** in the right direction."*

Turn toward your office and go. What's in it for the customer? You are respecting their time and after a few quick questions, they'll see what they came for.

Using the word 'us' is important. It conveys the message that you and your customer are a team and you will be working together.

Bring the customer to your desk. This sets the pace for you to be in control. Now you will have more opportunities to build on the relationship. You can bring them into your world by using the guest sheet.

Chapter 4

Are you afraid of the guest sheet?

Guest sheet

Are you afraid of this part, the taking of personal information? Most sales people are, although they rarely admit it. Taking personal information can be a very scary and tense situation.

Working from fear is one of the biggest restraints on sales people. All of our sharpness and natural instincts are stifled when we work from fear. This is why the W.I.T.H technique is so very important.

The guest sheet should be used to continue building the relationship with the customer. Have them continue talking about themselves. This may seem strange to the customer if they never experienced a sincere salesperson that did not use sales tactics from the beginning and may initially cause them to be cautious. Once the shock and reality of your ease and sincerity sinks in, this will subside. When it does, you will have a solid foundation on which to build.

Open Ended Questions

While using the guest sheet, you should be finding out more about the customer: what they do for a living, what they like to do when they're not working, if they have any children, if they're married, what they like about the car they are presently driving, what they would like in their new car, etc. Keep the customer talking and keep the flow of conversation smooth.

This is done by asking open-ended questions. You can ask for a work number, which leads into what they do for a living. You could then ask how they like what they do for a living. This is how you get a real sense of what the person is about.

If you are working with a couple, find out about both of them. For example, how did they meet and how long they have been together. Engage everyone in the conversation. You don't want to prejudge who the decision-maker is and then later find out you were wrong.

The information obtained from the guest sheet will help you find out what the customer's needs and wants are and how it will fit their lifestyle. You will be surprised how this information can assist you in building a strong relationship and, ultimately, help you sell your product.

Do you think of yourself as a problem solver or as part of the problem? It is so easy to be portrayed by the customer as the problem. Customers often feel that sales people are a necessary evil that must be dealt with and not by any choice of their own. If your customer thinks of you as a problem solver, rather than the actual problem, do you think you and your customer would have an easier, more pleasant experience? Of course you would. You will also maintain a higher gross profit and have happier customers.

Learn the customer's purpose, find out their challenges, and help them solve their problems and fulfill their needs, both monetarily and emotionally. This is achieved by asking appropriate questions.

Open-ended questions begin with the following:

WHO?

WHAT?

WHEN?

WHERE?

HOW?

WHY?, however, should be used with caution because it often has a confrontational tone. For instance,

"Why are you considering this type of vehicle?"

This question will most likely cause the customer to become defensive because they feel they have to justify their choice.

Try this instead:

"How does this vehicle fit your needs?"

Using these words will help you find out the true needs of the customer while maintaining the comfort of the customer as well.

The following are examples of non-confrontational open-ended questions;

"What are some of the most important features your next car will have?"

"Who will be doing most of the driving?"

One of the most powerful series of questions you can ask a customer is,

"How long have you been considering buying a new car?"

"What brought it to a head?" and *"Why now?"*

The reason this series is extremely effective is because you are finding out the true purpose and not just the reason. You will also find out if they have shopped at other stores, etc.

Furthermore, this information will help you later on in the sale when you present the features and the strong points of your product as they relate to the customer's needs.

Reason vs. Purpose

Every customer has a **reason** for buying a new car and most sales people will find out this information. However, there is something far more important that most sales people will not find out. What is the customer's **purpose** for buying the car?

Example:

A mother and father are buying a car for their daughter who is going away to college. The reason, which is quite clear, is that she will need transportation. But what is the purpose of buying the car? Most likely, they love their daughter and want her to have a safe, reliable car that can be serviced locally where she is attending school. As a result, her parents will feel at ease.

How many sales people actually tap into the emotional part of the experience? Customers will talk about these things if you engage them. If you do this, you become a friend and an advocate. You are then seen as a problem solver, instead of the problem.

There are hundreds, possibly even thousands, of situations why people need or want to buy a new car. Do you ever know the customer's true purpose? Do you care to find out?

"Every customer has a reason and a purpose for buying something."

"Find out their true purpose and you have earned the right to ask for the sale."

Always Be Confirming

Now that you have found out what you need to know about your customer, always confirm that you understand what is important to them. This technique has many purposes.

1. Your customer will be agreeing with facts they have already told you about themselves and, therefore, they will be responding "**yes.**"
2. Since you understand their needs, their comfort zone with you will increase.
3. You will know that your customer is in stride with you.

Many sales people make one common mistake. They go through their entire pitch without knowing if their customer is with them mentally until the very end, which may then be too late. Many customers will yes you and nod their head and this is taken as if the customer is truly interested in what you are saying. Because of the fear of rejection, most sales people will accept the head nodding as a yes rather than face the objections as they arise. In other words, you need to close the door each time you take a step in the sale to ensure that the customer is beside you each time. *"Always be confirming"* will help you to accomplish these tasks.

Some examples of confirming phrases are,

"If I understand you correctly..."

"So what you are saying is..."

"It sounds like you..."

Implementing such phrases helps you obtain accurate answers to all the important questions regarding price, features, etc. It helps you to show the correct car and then sell the features and benefits that fit the exact needs of your customer.

If you can secure this information up front, then you are in control and on your way to a sale.

Surface selling

Surface selling is when superficial information is simply exchanged between a salesperson and a customer without getting to the meat of the sale. Are you a surface seller?

The skin of an apple can be colorful and enticing, but it is only when you take a bite that you can taste the sweetness.

Do you show your customer, in the most simple and effective ways, how they will benefit from choosing you and your product?

Let's say a customer is comparing a lease to a buy. Do you give them both payments and wait for a response or do you show them the benefits of one or the other?

Many sales people find out the information needed to land the customer on the right product. They can even present the ideal payments. Everything seems perfect, but what is holding the customer back? The answer is that they are not sold on you and your organization. It is not enough in today's competitive market to simply make the numbers work for a customer. They want and expect more.

Why you? Why your dealership? If they can buy the same product closer to home, why should they buy from you?

The answer is below the surface.

What has greater value, a package or a single item? If you, your service, and the testimonies of dozens of customers come along with your deal, do you offer a better value at the same price? Of course you do. This is what selling below the surface is all about.

OK, so you have a Toyota Camry, but so does Home Town Motors. Dig below the surface and show the customer why they should do business with your organization.

I believe that visuals help break through the surface of selling. For instance, take your customer into your service department and show off it's size and cleanliness. Bring your customer to your inventory board to show them how scarce the model is they are looking for, which will create a sense of urgency. Be creative by using the resources available to you to make a statement that will enable you stand out from the crowd. You've heard the saying, "go beyond to earn the customers business." I say "go below and earn the sale."

"The skin of an apple is colorful and enticing…

But it is only when you take a bite that you can taste the sweetness."

Recap

- Disengage the customer's Force Field
  Decode what they really mean and
  Don't scare them
- Stop Selling
- W.I.T.H
  Focus on small talk

  "How much time did you plan on spending with us today?"

  "To make the best use of your (amount of time), *let me ask you a few quick questions so I can point* ***us*** *in the right direction."*
- Guest Sheet
- Open Ended questions
- Reason vs. Purpose
- Always be confirming
- Surface Selling

Part II

The Seven Commandments Of Selling

1. Land on exact product
2. Empathy
3. Make a friend before you insult
4. Stay high and make it look difficult
5. Feature, Function, and Value
6. Sincerity
7. Control

Is your goal to sell cars,
increase gross profit,
and work with less stress?

The Seven Commandments
of selling are the tools you will need.

If you only do four out of the
seven commandments, you lose.
You must do all seven. Each is as
important as the next.

Chapter 5

Commandment 1

Land on Exact Product

Land on exact product

It is so easy to confuse a customer. When you do, it not only engages their force field, it also assures you a, *"let us think about it"* response.

I have met some very good sales people having the gift of gab and a winning personality. However, what separates them from the real professionals is their lack of ability to control the sale and set a goal for themselves and their customer.

Selling is a series of victories eventually leading up to the sale. Once you have established rapport, you must find out exactly what product you will be selling. This may take some time however, so be patient. You must find out their needs and wants, as well as your customer's budget, time frame, etc.

If you start negotiating on a fictitious product, you lose. Whether in stock or ordered, you must find the exact model, options, and color.

How is this accomplished? Most sales people will either be too direct or too vague when it comes to finding out a customer's budget. You have already found out what product they have. You have built a relationship and opened the lines of communication. However, remember that the relationship can turn on you at any given moment. Therefore, you must keep in mind that your customer is always thinking, *"What's in it for me?"*

If you ask a customer how much they want to spend, what are the most likely responses? What is the customer thinking? First of all, did you earn the right to ask that question? Do you have the customer in their comfort zone? If not, expect engagement.

How much a customer wants to spend is an intimidating question. To you it sounds like a pretty simple and fair question, however, your customer may think you want to know so you can conveniently find a car that fits that price.

Remember, to a certain point you are perceived as the enemy and they are looking for your ulterior motive. So what can we do? Using the correct verbiage at the appropriate time will work miracles. And remember, what's in it for them if they share this information with you.

Try this:

"Mr. Roberts, give me an idea roughly what you are comfortable with as far as a monthly payment. Not a commitment, just an idea so I can point us in the right direction."

If the customer says they do not know or they haven't thought about it, then you must go further to show them *what's in it for them,* if they provide you with this information.

For example,

"The reason I ask is so that I won't show you a car you will fall in love with that doesn't fit our range or so I won't overlook something that will work perfectly."

What's in it for them to answer you? First, you took the pressure off by saying roughly and not a commitment. Second, by sharing this information and telling you the truth, they will see the cars that fit their budget and not waste their time. Plus, customers do not want to lose out on the perfect car by not sharing this information. This strategy works wonders. It is very simple, but rarely used correctly. Once you have mastered the implementation, you are then perceived as a consultant and friend and not as a Sales Rep.

Do you think it's important to find out the customer's budget? More important than you can imagine. Keep in mind it's not what you ask, but how you ask it that matters.

What other information could you use up front that would benefit you during the sale? I'm sure you can think of dozens. Try this technique for all of them.

"The difference between
Pressure and Persistence
is technique."

"The difference between
Pushiness and Assertiveness
is Technique."

You'll be surprised how easy it is to find out important information from customers; information most sales people would not dream of asking.

I was once involved in a deal where the General Manager of the store was 'taking over' (T.O.ing) a customer for a salesperson. This went on for about 45 minutes and then the General Manager asked for my help. He was stuck with a maybe offer at $9,500.00 on a car, which represented a $400.00 loss. He had no commitment from the customer. He did not know, nor care, where she came up with this offered price. Why was she so inflexible? They were at a stand still with the customer and I was asked by the General Manager to help close the deal.

I was introduced to the woman and her husband. She did all the talking and was clearly the decision-maker. I spent the first few minutes making them feel comfortable. I was now the third person trying to close the deal. I did not ignore her husband, as I wanted him as my ally.

I explained how I respected them for looking for their best deal and that they had the right to do so. I told them this was why I was now involved and that we wanted their business. Within one minute, she pulled out a buyer's order from her pocketbook from another dealership a few miles away. She now felt comfortable enough with me to share their secrets. Within five minutes, we took her receipt from the other dealer as a souvenir and sold her our car at a higher gross than she originally offered.

What was different about what I had done? No selling. No pitching. Just getting inside the customer's force field. We, as sales people, must be able to find out the true core of what the objections are and why they exist. This particular customer did not feel it was in her best interest to share this information with the General Manager. However, she felt it was important to share it with me. This was the key to earning her business.

This is the magic of Non-Confrontational Power Selling. The technique is subdued while the results are powerful. This is what we are in the sales business to accomplish.

What other information do we need to find out to help land a customer on an exact product? We talked about open-ended questions. What they liked or disliked about their current car, etc. Every technique is used throughout the sale.

Let's go through another situation. You are sitting with a customer for awhile and you believe you have established good rapport, but you cannot land them on an exact car. Maybe they're being vague as far as what the car will be used for or maybe they keep asking you how much this is and how much that is. I am sure you are familiar with this type of customer. They are bouncing from car to car and you feel you have two options. One, ask your manager to take over the deal or two, let the customer go and answer your manager's endless questions. Being in this situation is very common, especially in a used car department because of the enormous choices customers have.

Let me share something with you. There are an infinite number of reasons why people will not easily land on a car. For example, maybe the customer has recently married and must now leave the sports car world behind, but is reluctant to do so. Maybe the customer has a credit problem and the last dealer could not get them approved on the type of car they wanted. Now they're apprehensive about telling you what they want. Pressure tactics are the biggest reason of all. Once a customer lands on a car, they know the painful task of negotiating will begin.

This is why we need to make them feel comfortable enough to share information. Acknowledging that this occurs is the first step to overcoming it. You must not accept that all these people are *"just looking."*

Chapter 6

Commandment 2

Empathy

Empathy

I would like to introduce to you the most important word in sales, Empathy. I believe without **empathy,** you have nothing.

Why is this word so important? Extending empathy connects you to the customer in a way that words cannot describe. Empathy is the bond.

Consider this example

It's your first time sky diving and you are about to jump out of an airplane. Which scenario would make you feel more comfortable and at ease?

The instructor says to you, *"This is easy, just do it. It's not a big deal."*

Or

The instructor says to you, *"Oh, I remember my first time. I was so nervous, but the rush I experienced helped me overcome my fear. Just be in the moment and trust in my experience to keep us safe."*

If you have not chosen the latter, please choose a field other than sales!

Your customer needs to hear reassurance. Can you learn to identify the magnitude of their situation? Are you able to make them feel you understand their concerns and they're not alone in feeling that way? Reassure them that you are there to walk them through the steps safely.

Empathy is used throughout the sale. It is most important when trying to land a customer on an exact product.

Many sales are lost at this point. A salesperson asks the customer, *"what type of car are you considering?"* The customer says, *"I haven't really thought about what type of car. I just know that I need to replace mine."*

Typical response by a salesperson... *"Two door or 4 door? Stick or automatic?"*

This does not address their true initial concern... **You.**

Try this... *"Yes, I know how confusing it can be with all the choices available today. Why don't we figure out what is important to you and then we can figure out which direction to go. How does that sound?"*

You reassured them that it's all right to be unsure and that you're willing to spend the time to help them through the steps.

It is truly amazing what is accomplished by changing your sales approach from pitching and qualifying to mentor, consultant, and advocate. The problem is that most sales people are not comfortable in this role and this is portrayed as such to the customer. The vicious cycle continues.

Empathy is not sympathy. You do not want to alienate the customer by making them feel bad. Empathy is only effective when it is from the heart. You can use it when needed and still be sincere.

Most people have a natural ability to be empathetic. It is used throughout life. It soothes and relaxes a person. This should be your immediate goal with a customer. When used in its natural state, empathy has an almost magical effect. It's like a warm blanket for the soul.

Let's say a customer is shopping for a car and they seem distant and unemotional. Most sales people do not know how to handle this type of customer. The customer can be perceived as uninterested to the untrained eye. Stop selling and confront this in a gentle manner.

Example, ask a customer:

"How have you found the experience of shopping for a car?"

More than likely in one way or another they will say that it's horrible and they can't wait for it to end.

You follow up with:

"Yes, I've heard that many times from my customers. It starts off fun and becomes a burden. Is this how you feel?"

They will usually elaborate and give you an example of their experience. This is good. Although sales people do not want to hear it, this builds the bond and gives you an idea of what turns them off.

No matter what stage in the selling process you are in, empathy works its magic.

If a customer cannot commit during your close, explain that you understand how difficult it is to make such choices. This will allow you to go through the steps of summarizing the reasons this is the deal for them, without engaging their force field. Even if a customer cannot decide on a color or whether to use your financing, empathy has an affect.

Practice using empathy by role-playing. As sales people, we are so geared towards selling that we do not hear some of the elements that are key to the sale.

Recently I held a training class on being aware of when empathy could be used. I had the sales people role-play scenarios that would be conducive to using empathy.

One salesperson role-played a recently divorced customer. He explained how he wanted to trade in the mini-van for something sporty because he wanted to have fun and live again.

He displayed anger towards his ex-wife by saying, *"The hell with her, I am doing this for myself."*

The salesperson then asked, *"What type of sports car?"*

He missed the greatest opportunity in the world.

He could have validated by saying, *"Divorce sounds like a tough challenge. I can understand why you would want to put your own needs first."*

Or if appropriate, he could have shared a personal experience by saying, *"Oh, how I remember going through that myself. That was rough. I understand your need to take care of yourself now."*

Empathizing with emotions opens opportunities for building a strong and trusting relationship. Being real is a good thing. Don't be afraid to ask personal questions. Empathy is like a warm blanket for the ego. People will share emotions, provided they feel comfortable.

Using empathy to control the negotiation

During the negotiation it is possible the customer may become suddenly nervous, This usually causes the customer to change gears very quickly in order to try to gain control of the sale and try to remove themselves from this uncomfortable situation. This may be because they are beginning to feel the reality of having to make a decision. Many sales people will panic if they have lost control. Sales people must keep their cool at this point. This is the customer's way of testing you one final time before they jump into your arms.

Usually a customer will say something like *"I really need to sleep on it, are you in tomorrow?"* These comments can knock you off your stance if you are not ready to handle them comfortably. This is why you must be prepared at all times.

One of the best ways to handle this is to once again reassure the customer by validating what they are feeling. Example:

"I sense that you are feeling a little uncomfortable. I want you to know that if you weren't nervous you wouldn't be normal. Not many people come in and say, sure, write it up. It is a big decision. But what is nice is that I earn people's business when things make sense. When they like the car, are being treated fairly and find someone they would like to do business with, that's when I earn someone's business. I feel we have accomplished all these things. I am comfortable and feel that you are as well. Am I correct?"

What we have we accomplished by using this verbiage? Let's take a look. First you validated their feeling. You did not alienate them. We also summarized the main reasons people do business with you and verified that you have collectively accomplished these together. You have used empathy together with a Non-Confrontational way of asking for the sale. At this point you will shake out the real objection, if any, and proceed with the process.

"Genuine empathy is like
a warm blanket for the ego."

"It can bring you and
the customer closer in a way most
sales people cannot imagine."

Chapter 7

Commandment 3

Make a friend before you insult

Make a friend before you insult

I can recall six years ago hiring a salesperson named Roger. He had about five years experience in auto sales and considered himself a professional. His grosses, however, were considerably lower than the rest of the sales people that had been working my system.

I explained to him that his grosses were low because he wasn't asking for higher ones. I asked him to try to quote all of his customers at list price. He responded by telling me that he felt the customers were too intelligent to pay list and he would be insulting them. I asked him to try it anyway and he agreed.

When Roger's first customer sat down at his desk, he quoted list price on a new 1993 Buick Lesabre. The customer stood up and walked out on him. He came to me and said, "You see what happens when you quote list price. He walked out on me." I asked him what he did prior to quoting the price. He said, "the customer was looking for the Lesabre and asked for my price. I gave it to him and he left."

It's true that quoting list price can be perceived as an insult, especially to an educated buyer who has been shopping around. So what do we do? Discount every car, every time? Try to prejudge who will pay list and who won't?

First of all, you do not have to make excuses for asking list price for a car. That is the manufacturer's suggested retail price. Getting a discount should be an exception to the rule.

So I asked Roger to try something different next time. I suggested he stop selling and forget the car and the price. I recommended he talk to the customer about themselves; how they heard about us and what they enjoyed doing when not shopping for a car. (Remember, W.I.T.H) I explained that once he learned about the customer and had a common bond, he should come see me for further guidance.

When Roger met his next customer, he did just as I asked. For the first three minutes, he engaged in good conversation with the customer. It just so happened that the customer was a bartender. This was a very good bond, since Roger owned a restaurant prior to working in the auto business.

When Roger came to tell me about their conversation, I gave him the list price for the car his customer was interested in. Roger went back and quoted the price on the 1993 Buick century. The customer then said, *"Come on Roger, I found the car at another dealership for $1,300.00 less. You can do better than that."*

Alleluia! What goals were achieved? Roger now knew where his customer had shopped, the price he was quoted, and that his customer really wanted the Century. Since they had established a bond, the customer not only stayed, but also told him every objection up front. Plus, they were on a first name basis. He made a friend before he insulted the customer. The results were extraordinary. This is Non-Confrontational Power Selling at its best.

Once you've established a relationship, you've earned the right to guide a customer through the sale. Whether a customer is angry or scared, making a friend enables you to control the sale. If you told a stranger in the street that you didn't really like what they were wearing, what would be their response? What would be the response if you shared the same comment with a friend? I can assure you the two responses would be completely different.

If you make a friend before you insult, you will rarely need to dig yourself out of a hole. The customer's true objections and concerns will come to the surface, as well as the solutions to address them confidently. It's extremely important to practice through role-playing so you can build the confidence needed in dealing with your customers effectively.

Chapter 8

Commandment 4

Stay High and Make It Look Difficult

Stay high and make it look difficult

Perception is equal to the value of a product. You can see this concept in newspapers, advertisements, grocery stores, just about everywhere. What does a customer perceive to be a good value? Is it the true best price or the one they think they earned?

When it comes to items that are usually negotiable, such as cars, homes, boats, etc., there are many theories and sales techniques to convince the buying public that your item is the best. I have heard them all.

I attended a sales seminar where the trainer was explaining how it isn't how much you give off the price, but rather how many times you do it. I have also heard others state that you should always give a discount to show good faith when starting a negotiation. They all have their merits.

However, my goal, as a salesperson, is to maximize my gross profit, as well as my closing ratio. You work too hard as a salesperson to give up any gross profit. There are enough professional negotiators out there. How do we keep control of them? How do we keep a professional negotiator at high gross and close them now?

We have already discussed *make a friend before you insult,* so you should have a relationship at this point. Keep in mind that while your goal is to stay high and make it look difficult, the customer's goal is to stay low and make it look easy. Therefore, it's important to not make the customer feel they're in a win-lose situation. This takes a certain technique; bringing a customer up in price is like going against gravity. Let me explain.

Every customer, although rarely admitted, has an idea what he or she thinks something is worth. Sometimes what they think something is worth is directly related to what they can afford. This causes the unreasonable offers that we often get.

Let's say you and your customer have found the car they want to buy. In their mind, they want to spend $19,500.00 and the list price is $23,000.00. The customer is figuring they can buy it for $19,500.00 because $3,500.00 is what their friend negotiated off their last car. If you originally quoted them $20,950.00, the customer feels that it's simply a matter of negotiating to get you down another $1,500.00 to their price of $19,500.00.

Your goal, at first, is to bring the customers expectations up. Staying high does this. You need to separate the difference between what they want to spend and what you quote them. If a customer is thinking $10,000.00 and you say $11,000.00, you have lost gross and will have a tough time closing this customer. Now they want more. You made it look too easy.

If a customer is thinking $10,000.00 and you quote $14,500.00, they might think to themselves, wow, I'm too low. Now their first price will rise to $11,500.00.

You may think it has a negative effect if you quote too high, but it doesn't. #1 Remember, make a friend before you insult. #2 People want something that is out of reach initially. It seems to be a greater value.

Doesn't $10,000.00 sound like a great deal when you started at $14,500.00?

The most successful sale I ever had was called a 'Slash It' sale. It was run by a company from California called Caliber Promotions. They brought the car prices way up and then had an exciting way of slashing the price to what was perceived as a great deal. It was still a $3,000.00 profit.

What do I mean by "make it look difficult?" Let's say you initially quote a customer a price much higher than they were figuring. If they like you, they will share with you what they are thinking. They will tell you that you're way too high.

What do you do now? First of all (you never know) the customer might agree to the first price. If they don't, explain this is the price that you have been selling the car at for quite some time and that anything less would be a great challenge and an exception to the rule. This again reinforces that they should not expect to get much more off the price. If they do, they will have scored. Remember, you must go against gravity.

At this point, a customer may even say the price is too much and they want to shop around. Most sales people would take that as a negative and lose control.

You must keep control and follow up with the Powerful Non-Confrontational verbiage.

Example:

"I can appreciate that you are looking to be treated fairly and I have never lost a customer because of price. It does seem that we are quite a distance from each other."

You must set the pace and the rules to your sale. You will ensure they get a fair price. But fair doesn't mean that they buy at the price they where initially thinking.

Never negotiate with a customer who is not willing to negotiate with you. Lowering your price is a waste of time if they keep saying no.

Use phrases like, *"I know you would be happy if I could do this price, but I can't. Therefore, I need you to help me so I can help you."* Always refer to your original asking price. This sets up for them to agree to negotiate. They may say, *"Yes, I would be happy at this price, but not any higher."*

Now you have a semi-commitment from the customer without committing to them. You don't want to make an offer to a customer. Never say, *"If I can do this, will you buy the car?"* The only thing this does is lock you into a price without a commitment from them.

Visuals are another great tool, especially when a customer is trying to knock you down and you keep trying to get them higher. Show them, in a simple way, that your goal and intentions are to be fair to both them and your business. The following example is one that my sales people and managers use with great success. It is simple and effective.

Take your left hand and put it approximately ten inches in front of your face, at eye level and plane level. Tell your customer this is what you own the car for. Then place your right hand about 6″ below your left. Now say *"If you offer me this, and I try to get you up here,"* (move your right hand to about 6″ above your left hand) *"shame on me."* Now bring your right hand back to 6″ below your left. Then say, *"But if you offer me this, and I bring us to an even playing field,"* (move your right hand even with your left) *"does this sound fair?"*

You have made your intentions clear and guaranteed yourself a 'yes' from the customer. This brings you far ahead in the negotiating process and builds an incredible amount of credibility.

Learning these techniques creates a less stressful and a more systematic approach towards successful selling. The bonus is that you can actually have fun doing it!

Here is a typical scenario. A salesman has a customer and is offered a price. He brings it to the manager, who hopefully, sends him back with a counter offer. Some very important things to remember are as follows.

Always leave whatever you and your customer agree upon subject to final verification. Get them to commit before you. Don't give the customer the opportunity to say yes or no. Never go back with a solid offer. Never go back with a sliding down scale offer.

Example:

"My manager said he can't do $14,500, but he said, maybe $15,000, maybe even $14,900."

This causes gravity to take control. As you go down in price, their mind are thinking, $15,000 to $14,900 is $14,700 and could be $14,600 which is really close to $14,500. Maybe I can do even better.

You must go upward.

Example:

"My manager said that price really isn't possible, but I told him to earn your business he must work with us. He said he will consider $14,900, $15,000 or $15,100."

First of all, $14,500.00 now sounds like the deal of the century. You will now get a much firmer commitment. Secondly, you will most likely pick up a few hundred dollars in gross. This technique is crucial in protecting against false commitments. There is nothing more frustrating to a sales manager than thinking he has a deal and then finding out he doesn't.

Chapter 9

Commandment 5

Feature, Function, Value

Feature, function and value

You now know what the customer is looking for. You know what is important and what is essential to them. You have found the car that best fits their needs. How do you present your product in a way that separates you from the crowd? Great sales people do many things to turn a prospect into a buyer. It is the true professional who can present his or her product in such a creative and effective way to fit the customers needs and passions.

Using the feature, function, and value system is the greatest way of marrying the customer's wants and needs to your product. If a customer had told you that he or she would be using the car as a family vehicle and planned to take trips a few times a year, it is important that you build your presentation around these points. For instance, the safety features, gas mileage, roominess, and versatility of your vehicle.

However, it is not enough to just tell the customer about these features. It is also important to explain how they will benefit from having such features and the ease of their use.

For example, if a customer showed an interest in the safety of a vehicle, how would you present the feature, function, and value system? Let's break it down.

What are the features? For instance, crumple zones and a drop out engine. Open the hood and show the features to your customer.

What are the functions? Explain that on impact, the crumple zones collapse the front end of the car to absorb the hit and the engine is designed to drop under the car so it will not be pushed into the driver and passenger compartment.

What is the value to your customer? Inform your customer that, even in serious collisions, they and their family will be as safe as possible. In addition, these safety features lower the cost of insurance.

This system demonstrates the value of your product to your customer, whereas if your competition does not use this approach, you will clearly have the advantage of earning the sale.

Let's say your customer is shopping for many different vehicles and they all have similar qualities. It is the salesperson that finds out this information and then clearly defines the benefits that will earn the sale. Remember one very important statistic that you will not find anywhere. **The sharpest person along the way gets the deal! Whether you are the first or last stop, if you fulfill the customer's emotional and technical needs, you will earn their business.**

Most cars today have a power seat. This doesn't sound like a very exciting feature, right? Wrong! It is in the explanation of the feature that grabs the customer. Is it just a power seat or *a 6-way adjustable luxury feature that enables you to get comfortable with the touch of a button? Whether you travel around the block or take a day trip, these power seats will make it more pleasurable.*

Sell, don't tell. A brochure gives dimensions and statistics, you, however, give benefits.

It's the end of the year and you have one car left. You have had it for many months. You know, that ugly one that has been in the back that nobody wants. How do you describe it to the customer? Do you say, *"I have one left, let me show it to you."* If this is what you do (or something similar) then you are losing business.

Try telling the customer, *"I think I saw one that just became available and I must check to see if it still is. It probably isn't, but let me check."* You then come back and say, *"Great news, it's still available and I am excited for you because it's one of the hottest colors this year. Let's go take a look."*

You make the difference in everything that happens. You cause the excitement and energy. Do you have to be a 'bounce off the wall' type of salesperson to have this impact on a customer? No. You just need to create the environment that is conducive to emotion.

Is it a blue car or *the 'new for this year' pearl blue clear coat?* Is it beige or *platinum mist, a color you never need to wash because it hides the dirt so well?* Then you rub your hand across the hood to show the dirt they couldn't see on the car. This is real world stuff and it works magic.

You have one car left and it is a popular equipment package car. It has power windows, power locks, cruise control, tilt, and a cassette deck. A customer walks in and says they want a basic car. They explain they have a limited budget and want to save money by staying with a bare car. Another customer walks in and wants a fully loaded car. A top salesperson will be able to fulfill both customers wants and needs with the same car.

How? To the customer who wants a base car, this is the basic package with mostly standard equipment. To the other customer who wants it loaded, you rattle off all the equipment, even the basic things such as power steering and power brakes, until you are short of breath. Remember, the sharpest salesperson along the way gets the deal.

Chapter 10

Commandment 6

Sincerity

Sincerity

How often do we communicate with people and feel the lack of sincerity? Nothing is more of a turn off to a customer than this. Your customer is anticipating this from the beginning. They're waiting for the plaid jacket, used car salesperson or maybe the politician of transportation. Be real careful you're not in these categories.

Most of the time, sales people seem insincere when they try too hard, use cliches or pitches they recently learned, or when they're being superficial. On the other hand, when you say something with sincerity, it melts into your presentation like butter. It solidifies any point you're trying to make. Can sales people have the ability to consciously choose to be sincere? Yes, because I believe that sincerity can be learned. One of the ways to learn sincerity is to take the pressure off you. This is accomplished by being confident; this comes from knowledge. In other words, learn this Non-Confrontational Power Selling program. Then you will not have to think about what you are going to say or how to plan your attack on a customer and you can be real. Sometimes this can be frightening, but by trying this approach, you'll be very surprised with the results.

Some key points of sincerity are eye contact, body language, and body contact. Let's say you're trying to make the point that the customer is being given a rare, special price. It helps to lean over the desk, lower your voice, and say with eye contact,

"There is no reason to have to sell this car at this price however, I understand that ***it is necessary*** *if I want to earn* ***your*** *business. The only thing I ask is that you refer customers to me and please don't discuss prices with them. I will treat them fairly."*

Wow! That was strong! Look at the messages you have given the customer. They are the only one getting this deal; not even their friends can get it.

You must use the correct body language when delivering these messages to your customer, all the time. Even when delivering a simple message, such as the following.

"Mr. Customer, do you know the only thing I would look forward to, for making you happy with this price? Future business. Please send me customers, that is how I will benefit from giving you such a fair price. Does that sound fair?"

Customers will usually respond with something like this,

"Oh, I sure will, you can count on it."

All they will do at this point is start selling you on the reasons you will benefit from giving them the price you did. **This firms up your deal!** This is exactly what you want to happen.

Two sales people can attempt to make the same point and yet, one will seem so sincere, while the other comes across as shallow.

Do you believe you sound sincere? If not, try this. Look in the mirror. Find something you like about yourself. Give yourself a compliment and notice how you feel. You should feel good about yourself. Now find something you do not like about yourself and still compliment yourself. You will probably feel bad. This works. You will see and feel the difference.

Do you know why you feel the difference? Because if you lie, you will not convince yourself otherwise. Don't practice being sincere by lying. This is not your goal. There is enough to work with by being honorable. Besides, customers will see through you. Does this mean that if you have a high gross profit you are lying to them about getting a good deal? No, because, ultimately, people will pay what they believe something is worth. If you and your service come with the package, then it is probably worth more to them than your competitor's product.

Sincerity is the glue that binds you to your word and your customer to you.

Chapter 11

Commandment 7

Control

Control

Undeniably, control is the most important aspect of the sale. Every sales trainer uses control, but the definition is often misunderstood. What does control mean to you? How do you know when you are in control?

I think of control as being the conductor, the leader, and the master of ceremonies. If your customer suggests something and it will not help you in your goal, then don't do it. Customers come in, all too often, and ask for a test drive within the first two minutes. Don't allow this to happen.

You must establish respect along with control. You can consider a customer's request and hold off on it until it benefits you and your goal.

Everything you have read so far in this book will help keep you in control. Control is something you earn. Do you know your product? Did you build the relationship? Did you gain the respect of the customer? Is the customer following your lead by asking questions and showing the correct body language? If you can truthfully answer yes to each of these questions, then you have control.

Most customers will try to gain control at the beginning. Why? They don't trust you. If you don't have control, it's because you fell short in the process and you lose.

A perfect example of lack of control is when a manager is brought in by a salesperson to T.O a deal. The customer starts off by saying, *"I just want you to know that he's doing a wonderful job."* Even though the salesperson smiles with pride, this is undoubtedly, an insult. This comment often means the customer feels safe and comfortable with you and in control. What they are most likely saying to the manager, in other words, is *"do not try to take control of the comfortable situation I have with my salesperson."*

Once you lose control, it is almost impossible to gain it back and any attempt to do so is an uphill battle.

Look for signs

Once you lose control it may be too late. You must be able to recognize the signs to avoid this from happening. As you have read, it is very difficult to take control of a customer who has had the comfort of setting the pace. So how can you assess if you are still in control? If you have a disease, it is the doctor's goal to catch it before it's too late. That should be your goal as well.

First of all, you can sense control. There is a different feeling between you and the customer when you are in control. Believe it or not, the customer would rather you be in control. They do not have the directions to get where they are going without you. But you must earn control.

If you are assisting a couple and they are at two different ends of the store, you are not in control. If you are working a deal at your desk and you excuse yourself to speak to your manager and as soon as you leave, the customer begins walking around the showroom, you are not in control.

Most sales people will accept this because they are just looking at other models. This is not true. A customer who is contemplating buying a $20,000.00 automobile should still be in heavy contemplation when you leave.

If you are working with a couple, this is their time to talk about you and their decision. If they do not remain seated, then you are losing control. Unless, of course, they are looking at the exact car that is being negotiated. It is that simple. When customers want to stand, it is because they are feeling vulnerable. This is a natural, built-in sensor for you. They feel sitting shows some kind of commitment to you and your time. They are correct, it does. This is why you must ensure control before test-drives and/or negotiations begin.

How to keep control

Keep it simple for both you and the customer. You are losing control because you have not answered the customer's big question, *"What's in it for me?"* The only way to possibly regain control once it is lost is to change gears quickly. Put your brakes on and change the subject. Be outrageously honest. Something likes this.

"You know, folks, I believe I have found the perfect car for you. I feel that you are comfortable with me and quite frankly, this seems like it really makes sense. I have been wrong in the past, so if I have missed something, please share it with me. It is important for both of us."

Or

"I am a customer myself and sometimes I don't want to hurt the salespersons feelings, so I hesitate telling them what is really bothering me. Please share whatever may be in our way, so I can try to make you happy."

Use this type of verbiage, no matter what the challenges are, to bring you and the customer closer together.

Control outside of your comfort zone

Customers, like all people, have distinctive personalities. Therefore, you must be able to adjust to each of them. I refer to this concept as the *comfort zone,* which we will discuss throughout this section.

Each salesperson has a certain type of customer that they work with best. The problem here is that the customer does not have to adjust to your personality, whereas you must adjust to theirs. If a customer falls outside your comfort zone and you are not equipped to handle them, your chances of earning their business are slim to none.

For instance, you are a quiet, laid back salesperson. If you are confronted with a take charge, controlling person, how do you handle them? Most sales people truly do not have an answer for this. Unfortunately, this is the reason why most closing ratios are low. If you could speak to only the type of person you are comfortable with, how would your closing ratio be effected? It would probably rise tremendously. Unfortunately, this is not the way it works in the real world. You are given opportunities and you must do the best you can. Smart managers will direct customers to the salesperson best suited for their personality type.

Customers typically fall into three categories. They are hostile, talkative, or quiet. Each type needs to be handled differently.

The hostile customer is the one who knows everything, has been hurt by a previous salesperson and probably starts off by saying something like,

"I just want your best price."

Most sales people will say something sure to cause confrontation. What can you say? Remember the force field. Think about it. It is so easy to make this an uphill battle. In fact, it already seems like one.

One of my favorite ways to handle this is to say,

"That's a good question. Let me ask you something. Would you recognize the best price if I gave it to you?"

There are only two answers, yes or no. If a customer says no, they will probably lighten up. However, you must not take away their pride. If you do, it will be conceived as a put down and will be counterproductive. To avoid this, you must follow up with,

"I'm guessing that you just want to be treated fairly, is that right?" They say *"yes."* Then you ask,

"How much time did you plan on spending with us today?"

What if the answer is *"yes"* to the question? What if they would recognize the best price if they heard it? You response should be confident such as,

"That's great. I always appreciate a customer who knows when they are treated fairly. How much time did you have to spend with us today?"

You now have control and will maintain it if you stay on task. You must stay in control no matter what. A hostile customer is usually the easiest to win over when handled correctly. They are also the most loyal when you have earned their business.

There are many situations we could discuss regarding dealing with hostile customers. No matter what the situation is, your immediate goal is to disarm them of their weapon, which is fear. This is usually why they are hostile. By understanding your customer, putting your emotions aside, and using the tools you have learned, you will win them over.

We disarm hostility by using empathy. Once again, empathy plays a major role in your sale. Whether a customer is hostile, talkative, or quiet, empathy will soothe them.

Now let's take a look at what happens when a quiet customer visits your store. They walk around and even after your W.I.T.H, it is very difficult to make any headway. What is most likely the challenge? They have also been hurt or heard something scary about you. Maybe they just hate the thought of being pressured.

You must confront the challenge, but do it without confrontation. The last thing you want to do is go with the flow and allow the customer to be in control, while ignoring the challenges, in an attempt to feel safe. This will only lead to no sale.

Example:

"Have you been having fun in your search for a car?"

Or

"Have you been searching long for your new car?"

You need to engage the quiet customer. These simple, non-confrontational questions will most likely spark a cord for them to share how they feel. It is their opportunity to tell you what they are thinking, safely.

Talk softly and give them space. Reassure them by empathizing how you understand the grueling task of shopping for a car. Give them an example of something you experienced so they can relate to you. Using third party stories is one of the most effective ways to make the quiet person comfortable in your environment.

For instance, you can explain to them how you feel when you are being pressured during the purchase of an item and how you wish you were handled differently. Another example is to bring up a previous customer of yours in a similar situation and how you overcame their challenges together. Make them feel comfortable by showing them you understand.

Staying in control means staying one step ahead. For instance, if you are working with a talkative customer, one who says they are buying a car today, they know more about your product than you do, and they tell you their life story in fifteen minutes. They then say thank you and leave.

A common mistake that sales people make is as follows. We are trained as sales people to get a customer talking. When we meet the talkative type of customer, we believe they are interested because they are talking to us. We think, "Hey, they like me." The truth is that they are in control and are likely done with you when they have no more to say or when you are no longer willing to listen to them. This is what I mean by comfort zone. You must be able to slow them down without insulting or stifling them.

Another example is when you ask a closing question or put a talkative customer on the spot, they change gears and body language real quick and/or become very quiet. You need to avoid this by taking control from the beginning. You do this by having them answer questions relevant to your direction. Let them use up some of their energy. Get and stay on task.

Something I like to do with a talkative customer is ask them,

"What is the one major goal you hope to accomplish today?"

Get them answering goal oriented questions.

Having a clear understanding of diverse personalities will help you handle them more effectively. Furthermore, you will be less likely to take things personally, which is a major reason why customers fall outside your comfort zone.

"Be aware of the changes in your customer's body language."

"Look for signs of anxiety, interest and approval ...and respond to it."

Your Comfort Zone

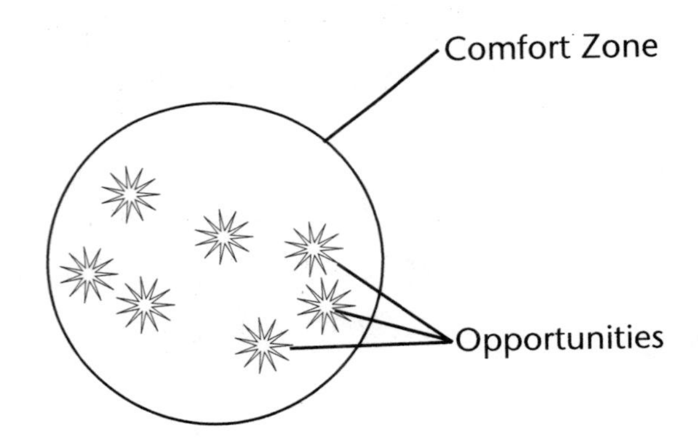

This represents the opportunities that fall inside your comfort zone

Opportunities outside your Comfort Zone

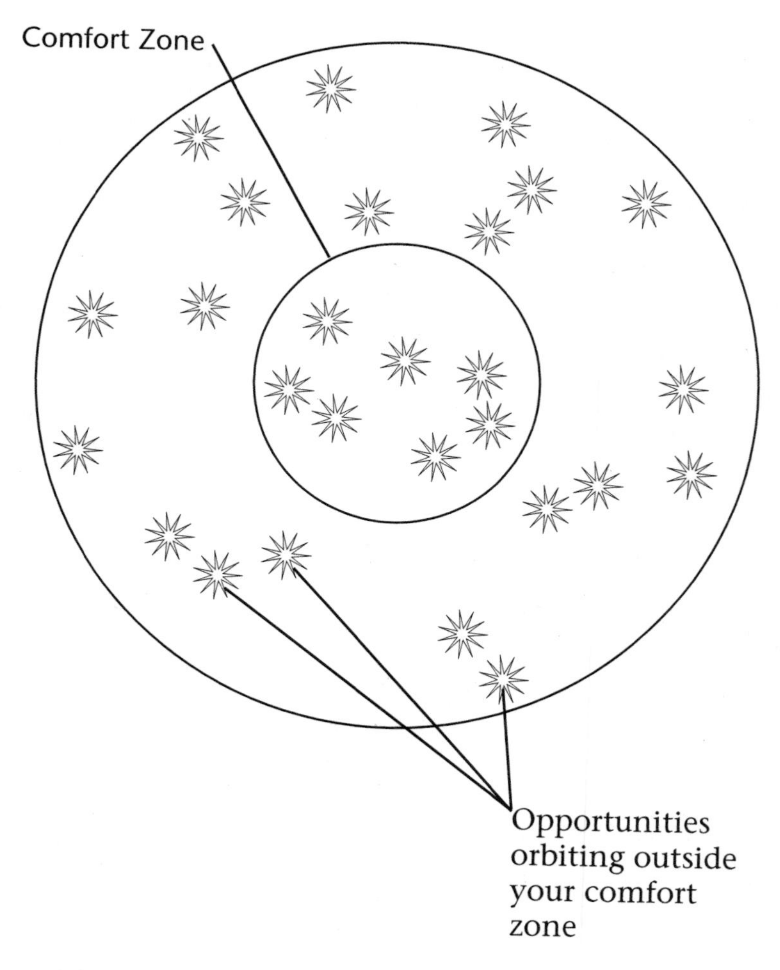

This represents the missed opportunities outside your comfort zone

New Expanded Comfort Zone

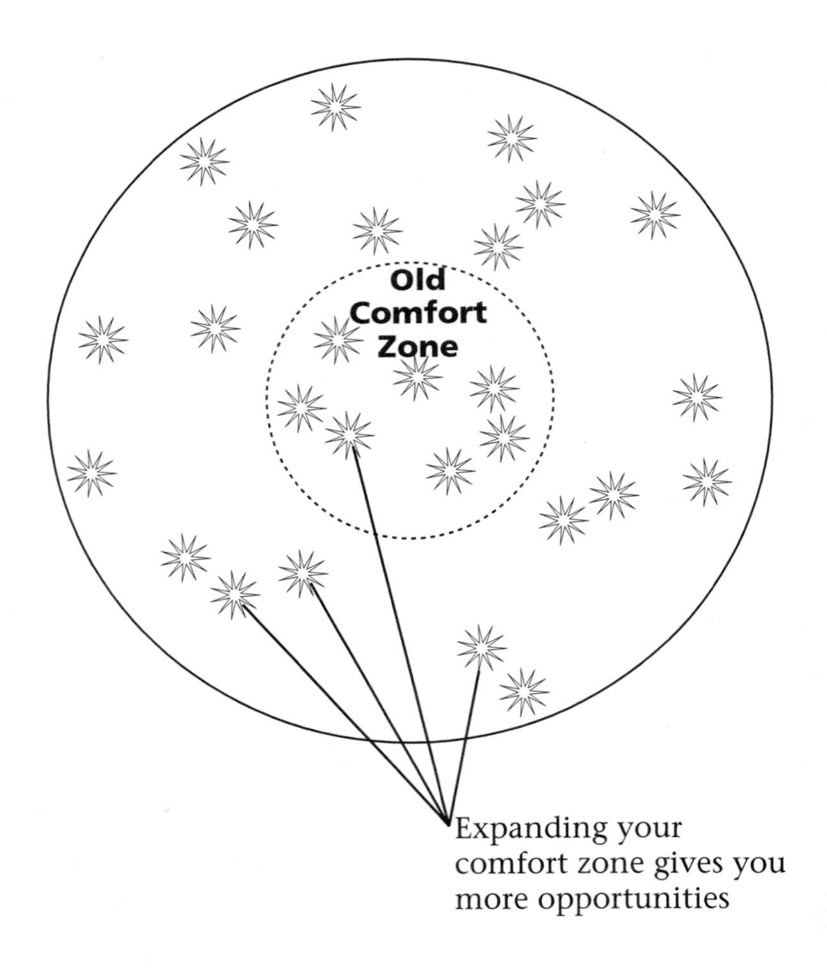

More Opportunities = More Sales

"You must expand your comfort zone to encompass more opportunities."

Part III

Non-Confrontational Power Selling Infrastructure And Tool Verbiage

Non-Confrontational Power Selling, Infrastructure And Tool Verbiage

- Disengage the customer
  Decode what the customer really is saying.
  Don't scare the customer.
- W.I.T.H (Welcome, Introduce, Thank and *"How did you hear about* (company name)*?")*
- Small Talk... about anything...
- *"How much time did you plan on spending with us today?"*
- *"To make the best use of your* (amount of time) *let me ask you a few quick questions so I can point* ***us*** *in the right direction."*
- Go to your desk. Have customer sit with you at your desk.
- Guest sheet (Use to find out more personal information, trade etc.) Even if no trade, what are they driving now? How do they like it?
- Open Ended Question

- Find Purpose. Ask

  "How long have you been considering a new car?"

  Wait for answer.

  "Why now?" And,

  "What brought it to a head?"

  This helps you find the purpose as well as the reason. Why someone needs a new car, it's easy to find out. How it will benefit or change their life is the purpose.

- Always be confirming
- Find out price comfort zone

  "Give me an idea, not a commitment, just an idea of what you are comfortable with as far as a monthly payment?" If they don't know, say

  "The reason I ask is so I don't show you something you fall in love with that doesn't work or not show you something that would work perfectly?"

  Also find out about the down payment.

  "How about as far as the money you want to put down. Again, not a commitment, I just want to show you the cars that will work for us."

- **Seven commandments**
  1. Land on exact product
  2. Empathy
  3. Make a friend before you insult
  4. Stay high and make it look difficult
  5. Feature, Function, Value
  6. Sincerity
  7. Control

About the author

The 35-year-old author was born and raised in Queens and on Long Island, New York. David is very excited about his first published book. He has been involved in the Sales Industry for over 20 years. He has written many training programs for the sales industry. Among these are programs on motivational selling.

David has been involved in many national training programs such as General Motors Dealer College. He has trained thousands of sales people, managers and owners for some of the largest national auto groups through his company Capital Results, Inc.

His dedication to learning and mastering selling has enabled him to reach his personal goals.

He brings to the sales industry fresh, innovative ideas, which are easy to understand and implement, even with the most difficult tasks.

In an age-old industry, he has had the ability to pioneer in many areas, which has earned him the reputation as one of the top national sales trainers and closers.

Sharing this information and seeing the effects of his training are his true passions.

Hands on, experiences and techniques are what he teaches. He believes that empowering sales people to truly understand the inner workings of selling will build the foundation needed for a long lasting, fulfilling and successful career.

His hopes in writing this book are to bring the caliber of sales people higher and to give the sales people reading this book a true infrastructure with which to go by.

To contact David Jacobson, e-mail him through *www.davidjacobson.com* or write him c/o Capital Results, Inc., 414 West Sunrise Highway, Patchogue, NY 11772.

Index

Order Form

If you would like to order additional copies of this book, please provide the following information:

Name ____

Business Name __________________________________

Address ______________________________________

City ____

State or Province ________________________________

Postal Code ____________________________________

Country ______________________________________

Credit Card Number: _____________________________

Expiration Date: _________________________________

Kind: ☐ MasterCard ☐ Visa ☐ American Express ☐ Discover

Please enclose US$16.95 for each copy plus US$3.20 shipping for the first copy and US$1.60 for each additional copy. New York residents, please add 8.25% Sales Tax. For orders over ten copies, please contact us for quantity discounts.

Send completed order form and your check or money order to:

Capital Results, Inc.
414 West Sunrise Hwy.
Patchogue, NY 11772
USA

or order via our Web Site at **http://www.BookaBuy.com**
Major Credit Cards accepted.

International shipping is extra. Please contact us for the shipping rates to your location, if outside the United States.

To keep informed of the latest projects and or to send your comments to David Jacobson, visit our Web Site at either *www.davidjacobson.com* or *www.BookaBuy.com*

For the largest selection of *Books, Cds, Videotapes or Computer Software,* Go to the Place That Has It All!

In Association with Amazon.com
and Beyond.com

Order Form

If you would like to order additional copies of this book, please provide the following information:

Name ____

Business Name __________________________________

Address ______________________________________

City ____

State or Province ________________________________

Postal Code ____________________________________

Country ______________________________________

Credit Card Number: ______________________________

Expiration Date: _________________________________

Kind: ☐ MasterCard ☐ Visa ☐ American Express ☐ Discover

Please enclose US$16.95 for each copy plus US$3.20 shipping for the first copy and US$1.60 for each additional copy. New York residents, please add 8.25% Sales Tax. For orders over ten copies, please contact us for quantity discounts.

Send completed order form and your check or money order to:

Capital Results, Inc.
414 West Sunrise Hwy.
Patchogue, NY 11772
USA

or order via our Web Site at **http://www.BookaBuy.com**
Major Credit Cards accepted.

International shipping is extra. Please contact us for the shipping rates to your location, if outside the United States.